SET FREE

SET FREE

A Collection of Spiritual Poems

Sienna Elizabeth Raimonde

Print information available on the last page.

Rev. date: 10/16/2020

To order additional copies of this book, contact:
Xlibris
844-714-8691
www.Xlibris.com
Orders@Xlibris.com
813506

CONTENTS

Dedication...ix
Foreword xi

Divine Intervention.. 1
All... 2
Behold 3
Today 4
For Me.. 5
His Eyes.. 6
Calvary 6
Self-Injury 7
Via Delarosa 8
Rebel 9
Help... 10
Abide 10
Found 11
Will You?... 12
City... 13
No Tears.. 14
The Beloved 15
Holy.. 16
He Cares.. 17
Depression... 18
Safe.. 19
Storm... 20
The Gaze 21
Pandemic... 22
The Walk 23
Silence 24

Grace and Power 25
Always with Me 26
Living Water 26
Faithful 27
One Day 28
Gethsemane 29
Seek 30
Bloodied 31
Quiet 32
Choice 33
The Cross 34
Why the Pain? 35
Amazing Grace 36
Complete 36
Jesus Wept 37
The Path 38
Beneath the Cross 38
The Imperceptible Presence 39
Fear 40
Addict 41
The Tree 42
Draw Me 43
Jehovah Raah 44
Drug Addict 44
Transparency 45
Overcomer 46
His Love 47
New Years 48
Saved 49
Easter 50
Mystery 51
Sought 52
Another Day 53
The Third Day 54
Wept 55
Soon 56
Believe the Bible 57
Before the Cross 58

Reconciled 59
Coming Again 60
The Glory Cloud 61
The Call 62
Set Free 63
Free 64
He Arose 65
Eternity 66
Redeemer 67
He will Abide 68
Transformation 68
Made Whole 69
Draw 70
Truth 71
Finished 72
It is Finished 73
Grace 74
Lost 75
Corn of Wheat 76
I'm Saved 77
The Seals 78
Holy Spirit 79
Waiting 80
His Call 81
Christ, Cross, Cornerstone 82
Emmaus Road 83
Alone 84
Agape 85
Sonship 86
Sons of God 87
I Will Restore 88
Pain 89
Name 90
The Valley 91

Dedication

After much thought and prayers, I felt to dedicate this book to my church in Kentucky, "Elk Lick Baptist Church."

Some years ago, my husband wheeled me into the church and I immediately knew that it was my church away from home. The love was unconditional and the message was straight from the Bible. I love all the people and, they have accepted me and my family with open arms.

"Set Free" is my fifth book, and I love to give out each new book to the people of my Kentucky Church. I love you all!

Sienna (Ps. 91).

Foreword

(by Sienna Elizabeth Raimonde)

The Presence of God is not affected by time. It is not seasonal, annual, or monthly. Instead, it carries the anointing to all who seek God's Face. It is "The Pearl of Great Price," "The Lily of the Valley", "The Light and Life" who carries us forward to our destination and causes us to finish the race. God's Presence cannot be bought, but only sought after by God's sons, His Bride, the Remnant, and all the Over-Comers who journeyed through the arid deserts until they reached Mt. Zion--The City of God. From there they went to the Outer Court, until they reached the Inner Court, and finally, The Holy of Holies. Yes, the Christian life is progressive. But, if we surrender to the Lord, His Presence will abide with us and, speak a word of victory to our souls. Allow God's Presence to be your treasure both now and forever more.

Divine Intervention

I walked along the shore one day
And there I met a man—
He seemed to know my inner thoughts—
He seemed to understand.

I asked Him what His name was and
He stopped and looked at me—
I AM the One and Only One
Who came to set you free.

And then He placed His hand upon
My head and I felt whole—
Whatever power He possessed
Was felt throughout my soul.

I turned to give my gratitude
But just then He was gone—
A flock of doves, flew overhead
While angels sang their song.

I never saw this man again—
I knew He was Divine—
He changed me from the inside out—
Salvation, now was mine.

All

I went to Golgotha
And kneeled at the cross.
My spirit was soaring,
My soul suffered loss.

I thought of the Savior—
He gave up the Ghost,
So, I'd be delivered—
He suffered the most.

I wish I could thank Him,
I held up my hand,
To show Christ I'm thankful—
My legs could not stand.

The Glory Cloud fell
As I clung to the tree,
Where Jesus was crucified
For you and me.

The Cloud felt so peaceful—
It shone, oh so bright,
As angels all gathered
Throughout the whole night.

And there I cried, holy—
My sins rolled away,
As Jesus appeared
As the Ancient of Days.

The Glory Cloud lingered,
For God gave His all—
Omnipotent Savior,
He hears when I call.

Behold

Behold His holy, risen name,
Which frees our soul from sin and shame.
The Savior puts His nail-pierced hand
Before our eyes to understand.

He searches high, He searches low,
Because He wants us all to know,
The reason why He came to die
Upon the cross, where He hung high.

He bore our sins upon the tree,
So, you and I could be set free.
He intercedes at God's right side,
In order that we would abide.

So, now we should behold His face,
So, filled with pain and our disgrace.
Still, brighter than the blazing sun,
He calls us still, to come—just come.

Today

Today the Lord came after me.
I did not know what I would see
But as the Master touched my eyes,
I could not see what I despise.

Instead, I saw the promised land,
And holes inside the Savior's hand.
I saw 10,000 angels sing
To Christ on high—my Everything.

And as he pulled me through the gate,
I saw the place where Adam ate.
But as I looked upon the tree,
It grew and grew eternally.

Still, in the distance I could see,
The cross where Jesus died for me.
And there upon His head I saw,
The crown of thorns He wore for all.

Just then the darkness turned to Light—
I marveled at this glorious sight.
Today I'm thankful—Christ, the Son,
Unites me with the Three-in-One.

For Me

I knelt beneath the rugged cross,
Where Jesus suffered pain and loss.
Then all at once I heard Him say,
I am the Truth, The Life, and Way.

There's nothing you could ever do,
To keep my love away from you.
But Savior you see all my sin—
And how your Glory fell within.

I give you all my heart and soul—
Forsaking sin, "Please make me whole."
That I might have eternal life,
To overcome all sin and strife.

And there before the Prince of Peace,
My jaded soul found sweet release.
Now I can ever praise the name
Of Christ who died that I might gain.

His Eyes

The only fire I shall see,
Comes from Christ's eyes to set me free.
Such Love will always be my choice
While I hear footsteps in God's voice.

His eyes are full of Love and Power—
Because it is the final hour.
Their beauty shines both far and bright,
While daunting folks embrace the night.

Whenever Jesus looks my way,
He turns my darkest night to day.
His eyes outshine the brightest stone,
Embraced by Love, You're not alone.

Calvary

I watched the Savior die for me—
He shed His blood on Calvary.
He paid the price for all my sin,
I bowed my head to let Him in.

The Prince of Peace was now my friend—
He stayed close by me 'till the end,
And when I felt like no one cared,
I knew His sacrifice prepared

My life with courage, strength, and power,
To overcome the darkest hour.
God's Glory Cloud encompassed me,
And filled my soul eternally.

Self-Injury

Here hair was matted, face was scarred—
And everything she did was hard.
She had no friends and only knew—
The mailman and two more—a few.

But no one stopped to say her name—
She felt so full of guilt and shame.
And in that place, she used a knife,
To cut her arms not take her life.

And when she saw the blood appear--
Anxiety would disappear.
And yet she knew captivity,
And longed that she would be set free.

Then Jesus came, His Love shone bright.
He washed her wounds and held her tight.
And there beneath the moon so bright,
She was delivered from the night.

Now Holy God—The Three in One,
Immersed her life in God's own Son.
His Love so great—His grace so free,
Bought my salvation on a tree.

Via Delarosa

The leather whips caused Jesus pain,
And yet, He never did complain.
While multitudes did mock His name
Although He took our sin and shame.

The road was full of dirty sand,
While Jesus fell—He could not stand.
So, Simon helped Him bear His cross,
Because the Savior suffered loss.

The Roman soldiers threw Him down,
And pushed sharp thorns upon His crown.
His mother cried and wondered why,
They placed Him on the cross to die?

He spoke some words then bowed His head,
While soldiers pierced His side in dread
To finalize, that He was dead—
The Son of God had died for all,
For every sinner since the fall,

For on the third day He did rise—
God had a plan which, some despise.
Still, it is written in God's book,
For all to see—Just take a look.

Rebel

I talked to God when I was three.
The pastor put me on his knee.
When I was five, and just a girl,
My spirit found God's treasured pearl.

A tiny tear fell down my cheek—
I found the Savior, kind and meek.
I knew the Holy Spirit touched my heart
And gave my soul, a fresh new start.

He promised He would never leave,
For Jesus saw I did believe.
He said that I was safe and sound,
While angels gathered all around.

And then one day, I walked away,
Although a gentle voice said, "Stay!"
I could not see The Light of Life—
In shadows deep, I now felt strife.

The Prince of Peace kept calling me,
You can't go back, and still be free.
So there within the forest deep,
The Savior rescued this poor sheep.

Together they walked toward the sky,
And all God's children wondered, "Why?"
The Lamb upon His throne forgave—
The friend of sinners came to save.

Help

I went to the waters to sit for a spell,
My life was performance and headed toward hell.
I pulled out my pistol and said a quick prayer,
As Jesus my Savior sat watching me there.

He quickly embraced me and there with a smile,
His Presence encased me—He spoke for a while.
I love you profusely and number your days—
Just give me your all and I'll teach you my ways.

You won't walk in darkness—My Presence—your Light,
To lead you to pastures and shelters of night.
Your life is not over—There's much more to do,
From now 'till forever My Love brings you through.

Abide

I walked through the shadows and there all alone,
I sat among pine trees, all covered with cones.
Then to my surprise the wind called out my name,
While Jesus my Savior, cast out all my shame.

His hand gently touched me, the Glory Cloud fell,
For Christ had redeemed me from eternal hell.
For there in the forest my Savior and King,
Revealed heaven's chorus, where angels did sing.

God promised that I would not stumble or fall—
The voice came from Jesus who answered my call.
From now on He'd keep me so close to His side,
For He will not leave me, but always abide.

Found

I tried to find the narrow way,
Where dark of night turned into day.
And all my pain, and all my sorrow,
Left my soul before tomorrow.

Then suddenly I felt a hand,
Which made me feel I understand.
And there beneath the autumn tree,
I felt my Savior beacon me.

His voice was tender—Soft and strong,
He made me feel I did no wrong.
His touch forgave me of all sin—
Because I let the Savior in.

His Presence glistened like a star—
So effervescent, near and far.
I placed my hands upon His feet,
And felt His scars but no defeat.

His blood-stained hands reached out to me,
So I would know that I was free.
When suddenly, He held me near,
To let me know—I need not fear.

Encased by Glory, raptured Love,
The greatest story from above.
Will be my song on heaven's shore,
Because the Savior loved me more.

Will You?

Before the great harvest comes to place
Are you aligned—amazing grace.
Before we're told to go outside,
Will you find somewhere safe to hide.

Before you see your dearest friend,
Will you decide life has to end?
Or will you take the Master's hand,
Who is the bridge to understand.

When this pandemic bows before,
The cross of Christ who says, "No more."
Will you behold the Glory Cloud,
While worshipping God's Son out loud?

And will you sing salvation's song,
To strangers who know they are wrong.
And if the darkness does descend,
Just ask the Lord that it will end.

The final harvest will not wait,
So, sons of God don't hesitate
To speak the Living Word this day.
For Jesus is the only way.

City

They chased me down the cobblestone—
My soul felt empty all alone.
I felt so cold and full of fear—
The sound of running feet drew near.

I fled down 52nd Street
And could not tell what I would meet.
Then suddenly I saw a door,
Encased by Light and so much more.

For deep inside I heard a voice—
Redemption's story, Victory's choice.
So, I said, yes! and took His hand,
Where Jesus helped me understand.

He is the Way, the Truth, the Life.
On Calvary He took my strife.
He shed His blood to set me free,
So, I would live Eternally.

And reign on high forever more—
I now was safe inside the Door.
The footsteps never entered in,
For they were covered deep in sin.

And, I was free to laugh and play,
Because the Savior made a Way.

No Tears

I cried the tears—He wiped them dry—
I felt His touch inside my eye.
I did not claim to understand,
Until I saw my Savior's hand.

A hole the size of dimes did shine,
Where nails once pierced this Man—Divine.
He whispered softly in my ear—
That I was safe and not to fear.

He touched my spirit, body, soul,
With Holy Light, He made me whole.
And as He gave me peace of mind—
I saw His essence—Love and kind.

And there beneath the Maple tree—
The Father, Son, and Spirit, three,
Brought violets by a pure, white, Dove,
Descending from the sky above.

My life is changed forever more,
Compassion does not keep a score.
But now I see the Light of Life,
Took all my tears and gave me Life.

The Beloved

I fell beneath the rugged cross,
Where Jesus suffered pain and loss.
My Savior never sinned at all,
But paid the price of Adam's fall.

He looked at me then shed a tear,
Because He knew the end was near.
I felt His blood fall down the tree,
Because He cared for you and me.

I called upon His holy name,
Until He took away my shame.
Right there, God's Spirit entered in,
Eradicating all my sin.

He reassured my aching heart,
And promised me He would not part.
But, said He's coming back one day,
To give His Bride a place to stay.

Holy

My friends smoked pot and snorted horse.
I watched each one fall off their course.
Then one day I beheld God's throne.
Since then I never felt alone.

The atmosphere—dense and opaque,
Was True and Holy—no mistake.
I realized then that God was Good,
And I could do the things I should.

So, I came back with Holy Fire,
And on this earth I heard God's choir.
For in my heart a holy song,
Persuaded me to do no wrong.

I pray for all my friends to see,
The Glory of eternity.
For if they will not say, "Come in",
Their fate is doomed to die in sin.

He Cares

I felt alone, misunderstood,
When suddenly I saw some wood.
It took me back to Calvary,
Where Jesus died to set me free.

I could not walk; I could not run—
I felt the Presence of God's Son.
And there beside the willow tree,
The Holy Spirit spoke to me:

I'm always with you, don't despair,
I will not leave you anywhere.
And when you feel so hurt inside,
My gentle Presence will abide.

Shake off the heaviness and sing,
To Jesus Christ the coming King.
For Yahweh watches far and near,
And speaks glad tidings in your ear.

Depression

I felt so sad I could not see,
The people all surrounding me.
I could not run, I felt so low
My mood was sinking down below.

I felt a band around my head.
My soul looked like the living dead.
I could not cry; I could not speak—
I soon became a living freak.

Then suddenly I heard a sound,
The Holy Ghost was all around.
My chains fell off, I now could see.
The Savior died for you and me.

I now could worship, raise my hands,
Proclaiming Christ to other lands.
The angels came, dispelling night,
While Jesus Christ gave Life and Light.

The Glory Cloud now covered me
And I rejoiced from sea to sea.
Let's dance together by His side—
For now, I know—The crucified.

Safe

I asked the Lord if He would stay
Close by my side both night and day.
The sirens blared—They sounded loud,
While voices screamed above the crowd.

Just then the Savior took my hand,
As if to say, I understand.
I felt abandoned on the cross—
The pain was great—I suffered loss.

And there upon the tree I cried,
While friends and foe screamed-- crucify!
Until the sad dark hour came,
Where God commanded, No more blame!

I paid the debt to set you free—
Forever you will dwell with me.
And now I'm living in your heart,
To give your life a brand--new start.

Storm

He is the Master of the storm,
Through good times and through bad,
If only you will trust in Him
He'll keep you from what's sad.

For Jesus saves your soul from death,
And heals your every pain;
Just give Him all your heart-felt wound,
And watch the Spirit's gain.

Forever more, He won't keep score,
Because He bled and died;
Now Jesus Christ gives Light and Life—
Our Lord was crucified.

Still, on the third day He arose,
That you and I Might live.
And as He intercedes for us,
He gave all He could give.

The Gaze

I saw Him look into my eyes—
His distant gaze was no surprise.
He reached down deep to take my hand—
This God/man He did understand.

He mitigated all my pain,
Then shed His blood that I might gain,
Forgiveness, pardon, healing too—
He saved my life because He knew;

Before the earth stood round in space—
My every sin Christ would erase.
And at the end of time I'd rise,
Triumphant in the bright blue skies.

I gazed into His sacred eyes—
Such colors I could not despise—
For in God's rainbow, red, orange, blue,
With yellow, green, indigo too,
Contained a promise signed by one—
The Sovereign gaze of Christ, the Son.

Pandemic

The days seemed dark—the future grim.
Still, Christians kept an eye on Him.
It would not take them by surprise—
The Bible spoke of Satan's lies.

The Father, Son, and Holy Ghost,
Were reaching out from coast to coast.
Coronavirus swept the land,
Each country did not understand.

Still, Jesus is The Prince of Peace.
He touched us with a sweet release.
And while His Presence shined so bright,
God's glory soon dispelled the night.

While thousands fell at my right hand,
God's Word stretched out from land to land.
And soon the Light of Christ did shine,
From coast to coast—It was divine.

The multitudes began to see,
The hope that shined from sea to sea.
The Blood of Jesus healed each soul—
The Light of Life will make you whole.

The Walk

I walked the creek until I met
A man whose eyes were deeply set.
His coat was white, like fresh, clean snow—
He seemed to know the way to go.

He spoke of life along the way,
And turned my deepest night to day.
I soon began to slip and slide,
Still, Jesus Christ stayed by my side.

He held me up until I knew,
His love and care would see me through.
And there I asked the Savior in—
To free my soul from shame and sin.

God's Spirit gave me Life and more—
He placed my feet on heaven's shore.
For now, triumphant I will sing,
Glad tidings to the King of Kings.

Silence

I sat beneath the old oak tree,
Where Jesus came to visit me.
The creek was high and flowing fast
To unseen places, far and vast.

I felt the Presence of the King,
And heard the angel choir sing.
I had so many things to say
To Christ who was the only way.

But there I felt the nail scared hand,
It gently said, "I understand."
For in the meadow, silently,
My Savior set my spirit free.

I did not speak—I just believed
That all my heartache, He received.
For there, beside the banks of shale,
God caused my hurting soul to sail.

Grace and Power

He looked within my soul and saw
A heart responding to His call.
I first repented of my sin,
And asked the Savior to come in.

My bloody hands were clean and white
While every stone shone through the night.
And there beside the crystal sea,
The Son of God called out to me:

"I am the Way, the Truth, the Life.
For on the cross I conquered strife.
And now together hand in hand,
Your enemies will understand."

"I paid the price to set you free,
And now you'll live eternally.
Within your mansion built by grace
Reflected in the Savior's face."

Always with Me

My Father is so good to me, I'm never left alone,
For when in loneliness I cry, He lifts me to the throne.
I never know just what to say, it doesn't matter much,
For all my problems fade away at my Father's gentle touch.

And when I get discouraged, thinking sin has blocked the way,
My heart begins to tremble and my knees begin to sway.
The One above who sees in love will quickly rescue me,
And cover my iniquities and set my spirit free.

Living Water

I went to the river and there heard a voice,
Of sweet melody singing, make me your choice.
I fell to the ground where I waited for more—
And watched while the angels all danced by the shore.

A scarred hand reached out, filled with God's loving care,
While a voice echoed gently, so holy and fair.
The waters will save you; they flow from my heart—
Remember I gave you a brand-new fresh start.

His Spirit lay heavy—I could not stand straight,
While God's Holy Spirit removed all my hate.
For there at the river Christ saved my dry soul,
While His Living Water made all my life whole.

Faithful

I could not walk or barely see,
When Jesus shined His Light on me.
The Word of God became my all,
And picked me up from every fall.

My knees were bloody, bruised, and sore,
While I lay prostrate on the floor.
The Bible said Psalm 91,
Would now encompass everyone.

And from that place of dire gloom,
The Holy Spirit filled each room.
The Father, Son, and Holy Ghost,
Were healing folks from coast to coast.

Until I stood on higher ground—
For now, I know I had been found.
The Blood of Jesus cleansed my soul,
Forgave my sin and made me whole.

For Jesus is The Prince of Peace—
And in His name, all war must cease.
My great Redeemer, King, and Friend,
is always faithful 'till the end.

One Day

One day my life felt despised and rejected.
One day my soul was in sin and despair;
Jesus came in and we made a connection,
Cleansed by His blood I was free of all care.

Now I'm secure as God's Spirit is in me.
Now I am free from my burdens and guilt.
Jesus, He saved me, I live with His Presence.
Now I am sure that my mansion is built.

Saved by His blood, He restored and forgave me.
Now I'm set free by the price that He paid.
Angels have paved, streets of gold up in Heaven.
God lives inside where foundations are laid.

Give Him your life, filled with hate and deception.
He will not fail you, just ask Jesus in.
Look in the Bible for help and direction.
Here on the cross Jesus cleansed us from sin.

Gethsemane

He prayed that He would never see,
The gruesome place—Gethsemane.
But God the Father had a plan—
The Blood of Jesus would save man.

Still, Jesus knew what He must do,
At Calvary for me and you.
So, as the blood tears trickled down,
The angels gathered all around.

And Christ surrendered all His will
In hope that God could now fulfill,
Salvation bought upon the tree—
A new creation, rich and free.

We cannot earn eternity—
The Blood of Jesus set us free.
A new creation, sanctified,
God paid the price when Jesus died.

Seek

I felt His Presence drawing near,
It cleared my path and chased my fear.
I felt completely whole inside—
There was no reason I should hide.

I opened up God's Word and found,
His holy Presence all around.
His love descended upon me.
His gentle smile set me free.

The Bible says to seek and find—
To ask Christ in your heart and mind.
For Jesus seeks His pure white bride,
So full of splendor, Glorified.

He knocks in answer to your prayer—
Just turn the handle, He'll be there.
The risen King has conquered all,
The things we lost when man did fall.

His Presence gives us victory—
He bled and died at Calvary,
That we would seek His unveiled face,
Until God's sons find changing grace.

Bloodied

I sauntered down a long, worn, path.
My soul was full of sin and wrath.
When suddenly I tripped and fell,
Upon my knees—I cried a spell.

My legs were bloodied, bruised, and scraped.
My life was full of pain, and ached.
I called on Jesus my new friend.
Upon His Word I could depend.

He touched my knees 'till they were whole.
Then, by His blood He saved my soul.
His strength was my redeeming place—
He filled my heart with love and grace.

My knees were now completely free.
The Blood of Jesus ransomed me.
My Savior, friend, beloved King,
Would be with me, through everything.

Quiet

In the silence by the river,
Waves are splashing to and fro.
I can't resist the chaos—
Only God can make it go.

Thoughts of anger, hurt, and trouble,
Pierce my senses—hurt my goal.
Holy Spirit, how I need you,
In the darkness of my soul.

Soon a Light beyond all measure,
Beckoned me beside the shore.
Jesus Christ the great Redeemer,
Gave me quiet thoughts and more.

How I love Him, how I'll serve Him,
In the quiet of the day.
I will never cease to praise Him,
Christ my Savior is the Way.

Choice

I made the choice to follow Him.
Through night and day—through thick and thin.
Through valleys deep and mountains high,
I heard Him call beyond the sky.

And there I saw Him sparkling white,
Bright colors came throughout the night.
I asked Him in—The Three-in-One,
Shined brighter than the morning sun.

I did not run; I did not hide,
I only said, "Lord, please abide."
And there I saw a rainbow rise—
Suspending colors in the skies.

I never will forget the day,
That God the Father came my way.
And in His Presence, I did rise—
A choice that made angelic cries.

The Cross

My life was saved in Jesus' name –
He paid the price, I'm not the same.
He bled and died to set me free-
The Sinless Man died on the tree.

My sin forgiven on the cross –
He suffered pain and so much loss.
The soldiers mocked the King of Kings
Who reigns on high, where angels sing.

Forever you will live on high,
Within the bright, blue azure, sky.
It only takes an honest call,
To save you from Edenic's Fall.

The Holy Spirit will come in,
To save your soul from Adam's sin.
And one day heaven's pearly gates
And streets of gold will emanate-
The cross where Jesus gave His all-
Redeeming sinners from the fall.

Why the Pain?

In the prison cell so dark and cold
The reason why is left untold
While doubts and fears present their case,
Such strain begins to grip his face.

He questions what was once so sure,
And cries for grace just to endure.
"Oh, where is Jesus in this place?
Deliver me from such disgrace."

The silence mocked his every plea
"If only Jesus I could see"
He sent messengers to find
The one who healed the lame and blind.

"John wants to know if you're the one—
Messiah, God's beloved Son."
"Go tell John what you hear and see
And not to lose his faith in me."

He didn't set the prophet free
Still, prophets don't die easily
His message still resounds today—
"He's coming soon- prepare the way!"

God never promised rosy skies
Or that He'd answer all our whys?
He said we'd have to take our cross
And every man must count the cost.

Though John was slain, I know he'll be
With Christ throughout eternity
And though I don't know why the pain
My faith beholds a greater gain.

Amazing Grace

Amazing grace will always be
My song throughout eternity.
For there, upon that lonely tree—
My Savior died, to set me free.

My knees both trembled in disgrace,
While blood rolled down His tear-stained face.
This blood it washed me white as snow,
And why He loved me, I don't know.

But as I stand before the throne,
Encased by grace, I'm not alone.
For on the cross, Christ bowed His face,
Then filled my soul with all God's grace.
No longer lost, In Christ I stand—
For by His grace, I understand.

Complete

God delights in what is best,
for at His feet, we now can rest.
We are saved by the Blood of the Lamb,
and restored by the great I Am.

The Holy Ghost will set us free,
While Christ the Son gives liberty.

The mysteries are ours to see,
while we bow down on bended knee.
Creation sings, in one accord,
for Jesus Christ, is now our Lord.

Jesus Wept

I felt a teardrop from above.
It filled my soul with God's great love.
He knew that I was falling fast,
And soon my body would not last.

I fell beneath a heavy load—
It was not silver, was not gold.
But sin that flooded every part
Of my unrighteous, hellbent heart.

And then the darkness pierced the night—
I could not see; I could not fight.
I called upon the Savior's name,
Confessing all my sin and shame.

Just then the angels gathered round
With singing full of raptured sound.
Because my soul let Jesus in—
Redeeming me of all my sin.

The Path

I went down a path that was wild and worn,
Then tumbled and fell 'till my legs felt so torn.
A Robin, Queen Anne's Lace, were all I could see—
I called out to Jesus, He called back to me.

I'll never forsake you, I'm close to your side.
I stay right beside you, just trust and abide.
He lifted me up where the poplars stood tall.
And there I did thank Him—my sweet all in all.

His hand was my anchor—So gentle and tight,
He did not let go for the path was not right.
I thanked my dear Savior, His love led the way,
To quiet green pastures—And bright sunny day.

Beneath the Cross

I left my sins beneath the cross,
Where Christ my Savior suffered loss.
And there the blood came trickling down,
'till I was covered all around.

The clanging shackles fell apart,
While God, the Holy Ghost did start—
A new creation, no more old—
My heart and soul became like gold.

You need to eat the Bread of Life,
For Jesus took all sin and strife—
He set me free from guilt and shame,
The day I called on Jesus' name.

The Imperceptible Presence

I traveled down a forlorn path, the trail was overgrown,
With every type of obstacle, I went there all alone.
The sun descended on the trail, I had to guess my way—
I could not bustle back on time or go another way.

My feet were sore, my limbs ached more with sounds inside my head;
I floundered without knowing where—I should have stopped instead.
Then suddenly I heard a noise and someone called my name—
I somehow recognized the voice, such comfort without shame.

He stood beside me lovingly He pulled the tall grass back—
To holograph an empty tree so nothing I would lack.
His hands scooped out some water from the creek that flowed nearby—
His kindness never ended so I had to ask Him, "Why?"

I watched you thrash about until I felt you had enough,
To go back home and overcome—for now, I know you're tough.
Not self-sufficient but relying on my Word and Power—
I'll see you through predicaments and through your darkest hour.

Fear

I did not think that I could be,
Strong and courageous, that's not me.
I did not think that I could climb,
Up mountains steep, or feel sublime.

I coward at the slightest thing,
Which made a noise or caused a ring.
And sometime in the night I'd hear,
An insect fly, it caused great fear.

Until within the dark of night,
Christ Jesus came and made things right.
He beckoned me to take His hand,
Although I did not understand.

He spoke my name and set me free,
Then face to face—empowered me.
My chains fell off—I screamed with glee,
Because the Savior spoke to me.

By pastures green you now can lay,
My Presence fills both night and day.
For now, you will no longer fear,
The dead of night—Your God is near.

Addict

There were no pills that could be found—
They saw me laying on the ground.
The pastor came and took me in—
I soon repented of all sin.

The gentle Savior pure and white,
Stayed by my side throughout the night.
And there I asked the Lord to stay,
Within my spirit—day by day.

Dear Jesus made the pain subside,
For there, my heart and soul both cried.
I felt the Lord, He entered in,
Eradicating all my sin.

I knew that I was free at last—
For Jesus overcame my past.
Until I sought His holy face,
And found sweet peace in His embrace.

The Tree

I saw Him hanging on the tree,
Because He came to set us free.
This perfect Man came willingly,
To show His Love for you and me.

They made Him carry His own tree,
Then nailed His body publicly.
The sky grew dark, the hill turned gray,
And then I heard the Savior say:

"Oh, why have You forsaken Me,
And let Me die on Calvary?"
His mother wept upon the ground,
While Pharisees stood all around.

And there He bowed His sacred head,
And saved the living and the dead.
When Jesus rose to heaven's shore,
His followers heard Him say more.

I finished all upon the tree—
Go tell the world to call on Me.
It's over now, I paid the price,
For every heartache, every vice.
For every pain and every sin—
Oh, won't you let the Savior in?

Draw Me

Draw me fast and draw me near.
Take away my every fear.
On the mountain way up high,
You ascended in the sky.

Let me see your eyes so deep.
Keep me close to your own sheep.
Let me hear the shepherds voice—
Help me make your holy choice.

You have died to set me free.
Now I'll live eternally.
Show me Lord that sacred place—
You forgave all sin, disgrace.
When you draw me, I will be
Clothed in splendor — Christ in me.

Jehovah Raah

I look to the Lord as my shepherd and friend.
He has no beginning and thus, has no end.
If I need protection, I call out His name—
His rod will protect me from evil and shame.

He owns all creation—I never shall need;
He gave me new life through His Son's sacred seed.
Jehovah Shammah is my keeper this day;
For Jesus, His Son is the Truth and the Way.

Drug Addict

I like to take a drug or two,
So that I know just what to do.
I ingest " H" Horse, Skag, or Junk—
Until I feel like I am drunk.

But that was not enough so I,
Took Xanax until I was high.
There was no help. I had no friend.
I felt like this must be the end.

Then I remembered Calvary,
Where Jesus Christ did die for me,
And there I knelt in utter grief
Until the Savior spoke relief.

And now I felt so clean inside,
Because God's Son was crucified.
And Christ forgave my every sin,
For I was truly Born-Again.

Transparency

Just tell the truth and ask Him in—
The Savior's death was so gruesome.
He died that you would live on high.
Through gates of splendor in the sky.

He is the Way, the Truth, the Life,
Eradicating sin and strife.
Yes, Jesus wants to be your friend—
The Savior will come back again.

The time is drawing to a close—
The final day, nobody knows.
But suddenly the trumpet blast,
Will tell the world it's time at last.

So, open up your heart this day,
And call on Jesus as you pray.
He does not need a fancy prayer,
For that will not go anywhere.
A simple honest upright call,
Will pave the way, God's Waterfall.

Overcomer

The Lord is holy, good, and kind—
He heals the lame and cures the blind.
He's oh so lovely—every day,
His Presence comes whenever I pray.

So, keep your eyes upon the race,
Because the Savior sees your face.
And when the going gets too rough,
The Holy Spirit says, Enough!

He never gives you more than you,
Are able to keep going through.
He lifts you up and makes you stand—
Until you say, I understand.

Just keep your eyes upon the Face,
Of Jesus our Redeeming Grace.
For God the Father sent His Son—
Who won the race for everyone.

His Love

God's love is deeper than the sea,
Much wider than the milky way;
And taller than Mount Everest
And longer than the longest day.

An atom bomb cannot compare
With how God's love is everywhere.
Pervasive as the air we breathe,
The calm of dawn—What we believe.

Assimilating right from wrong,
It beautifies all earthen song;
For this one attribute is more
Than everything we underscore.

It does not fade; it does not shrink—
God's love is greater than we think.
It will not change—It's not contained,
There's nothing like its vast domain.

New Years

I hope the new year brings us Love,
From Jesus Christ, our God above.
May every joy and every dream,
Be now fulfilled through the Supreme.

And if your hopes have not been met,
It's just a matter of not yet.
Remember how the Savior came,
To save our souls from sin and shame.

Now like a paper blank and pure,
We can be saved of this I'm sure.
Just put your life in God's great care,
And you'll find comfort everywhere.

For if you call on Jesus name—
Our gracious God remains the same.
So, let the Holy Ghost come in,
And Christ will free you from all sin.

Saved

My friend was saved, delivered too,
When Jesus told her, "I love you".
She did not need her Mary Jane,
Or pills to make her brain feel sane.

She felt God's Presence every day—
And walked beside Him all the way.
I needed Him within my heart,
To change my ways—It was a start.

So, there I called on Jesus name—
Until the Holy Spirit came.
To live inside my heart and soul.
I was complete—I was made whole.

I was delivered from all sin
Because I asked the Savior in.
He paid the price that I might live
And that is why I can forgive.

Easter

When Jesus died upon the cross,
He took my sins, disease, and loss.
Yet at the tomb on one sad day,
The heavy rock had rolled away.

The women wondered what took place,
Until they turned and saw His face.
Such Love enraptured every cell,
And now their lives were free from hell.

They could not wait but ran ahead,
To tell the rest—He was not dead.
So, Peter ran to check the place,
Where he had covered Jesus' face.

The tomb was empty—Folded clothes,
Lay on the spot where Christ arose.
The Lord is risen as He said.
Yes, Jesus is no longer dead.

Mystery

I went to the Bible
So full of God's history,
But while I was there
He surprised me with mystery.

The seals found in Daniel
Were now open wide,
I read God's own secrets
And that's where I cried.

The cross was ordained
Where the Savior would die,
While sinners were ruthless
And cried, "Crucify!"

The Savior died quietly—
After He said,
"Dear Father forgive them,"
Then bowed down His head.

They pierced through His side
To make sure He had died,
He said, "It is finished,"
Then sat by God's side.

The risen Lord intercedes
For you and me,
And soon He will come back—
Yes, all eyes shall see!

Sought

I searched for God through thick and thin—
Past all my goodness, all my sin.
The way seemed dark, I simmered sweet,
My feet were aching on the street.

I called out loud so He could hear—
I felt His holy Presence near.
And when I heard His still small voice—
My life was healed—I did rejoice.

My Savior led me through the night
And there He transformed all my sight.
The Lord drew near, my strength and might—
His candle called "I am your Light".

For there among the meadow green,
The flowers danced with joy unseen.
Christ took away the bad and mean,
For by His blood we'd been redeemed

And in the forest, I was found,
Where God's own staff led me around.
For there on Zion's holy mount,
My thirsting soul drank from the fount
Which lives within the secret place
Where seraphim's all bowed their face.

And one day we will understand
Our loving Father—hand in hand.
And intimate in every way,
Our Lord restored night to day.

Another Day

Another day, another year,
For Jesus to dispel my fear.
He does not live in time or space—
He died to give amazing grace.

He saved my soul and set me free,
His Love will always cover me.
He shed His blood on Calvary,
Where willingly He died for me.

There is a day of great despair,
Still, I will trust my Savior's care.
Forever I, am sealed by One.
I called on Him, God's only Son.

And there the Holy Ghost came in.
He saved my soul, dispelling sin.
I heard the angels sing my name;
It's all because the Savior came.

And on that day, I gave my all,
The God above did hear my call.
If you surrender at the cross,
Where Christ the Savior suffered loss,

You will see Jesus face to face—
Proclaiming every sin, erased.
Another day the golden gate,
Will open wide and not be late.

The Third Day

Jesus died upon a tree—
Suffered loss for you and me.
Only God can tell the plan
Which He chose for every man.

On the third day boulders fell—
You and I were freed from hell.
Jesus Christ arose where He,
Conquered sin eternally.

When we go through trials sore,
God almighty keeps the score.
On the third day all is well—
Jesus saved our soul from hell.

Sons of God now take your place,
Hand in hand you ran the race.
Reign forever—No more tears,
On the third day—Endless years.

Wept

Jesus cried in empathy of Mary and Martha's pain.
He knew their brother would arise—His death was not in vain.
They did not understand when He said, "Loose him—let him go—
Until He shouted, Lazarus!, Come forth so they will know."

"I am the resurrection Life—I give and take away,
I always loved you—You are mine—because I am the Way."
The crowd grew still while I embraced this man, I called my friend,
Because he said "I'll follow you and go where ever you send."

Then Lazarus gazed deep inside the eyes of liquid fire,
For there he saw a broken heart which cried out with desire.
"I gave my all upon the cross, and there in agony,
I suffered every kind of pain to set my loved ones Free."

Soon

It may be morning, evening, noon—
Our Loving Savior's coming soon.
Just as Christ ascended high,
We will meet Him in the sky.

Are you ready, Do you see?
He'll come back for you and me.
When the angel blows the horn,
Everyone who's been reborn,

Will be seated on white horses,
While the courts on high divorces
Any discourse from the fall,
Overcome by Christ, my all.

So, my friend, the day draws near—
Do not worry, do not fear.
Take your Bible to the mount
Drink from Him the Living Fount.

Believe the Bible

The Bible is a living Book,
I take it everywhere.
It soothes my soul and makes me whole.
It takes away all fear.

The "B" stands for believe in Me.
The "E" Eternal Life.
The "L" stands for the Love of God eradicating strife.
The "I" directs us to I Am—the One who died for me.
The "E" for enter in the gates, and live eternally.
Now don't forget the victor's "V"— He overcame the cross.
And gave His Life that we might live—The Savior took our loss.
Then finally, another "E", eradicating pain,
Because He hung upon the cross, exchanging loss for gain.

The Way is written in the Book,
The Bible tells it all—
For God will still unveil His Truth,
To creatures great and small.

Before the Cross

I stood before the cross and cried,
For there I saw the crucified.
He did no wrong—so why the pain?
He took my place and gave me gain.

He felt the nails in hands and feet,
So I could live free from defeat.
Then as He bled, I heard a sound—
His blood forgave all those around.

His mother fell, her heart grew weak.
She could not stand, she could not speak.
Then finally He bowed His head.
He finished all and bore our dread.

They put His body in a tomb,
For at His birth there was no room.
But on the third day He did rise,
To sit with Abba in the skies.

He's coming back, He paid the price—
For all my sin and every vice.
Yes, Jesus suffered on the cross—
That we might conquer shame and loss.

Reconciled

I felt conviction in my heart,
and knew I needed Christ to start
My soul again—I don't know how,
so, at the cross my knees did bow.

I then forgave both friend and foe,
and everybody I did know.
Just then I heard a gentle voice
say, "Child, you have made a choice."

For clinging to the cross I knew,
the Savior loved both me and you.
My burdens fell down at my feet.
my heart no longer, felt defeat.

The blood delivered all my sin,
for Jesus Christ had entered in.
So, if you want to be forgiven
remember where the nails were driven.

Coming Again

The skies were bright throughout the night,
While some deceased now gathered tight.
The trumpets sounded near and far,
And all beheld the Morning Star.

The prophets wrote so long ago,
Of signs and wonders we would know.
They spoke of darkness on the earth,
Which juxtaposed sons of new birth.

The moon would turn a crimson red,
And we would see the living dead.
The supper of the Lamb would come,
In honor of the risen one.

And all the earth would separate,
The ones who love from those who hate.
Look up my friend, He now draws nigh,
God tells the Truth, He does not lie.

He's coming back just as He went,
For Jesus Christ has now been sent.

The Glory Cloud

The Glory Cloud fell down on me,
So full of love and majesty.
It touched my heart till I was changed—
My inner being rearranged.

My soul was settled from above—
My spirit soared with God's great love.
The great I Am called out my name—
Enraptured I, was not the same.

His grace pervaded every cell—
His Omnipresence made me well.
The Glory Cloud is drawing near—
Eradicating all my fear.

The Father, Son, and Holy Ghost,
Anoint God's people coast to coast.
So, when you go to God in prayer,
You'll see His glory everywhere.
And when you bow before His throne,
The Glory Cloud will make God known.

The Call

I asked my Savior to reside
Within my heart and there abide.
Just then He came inside of me—
I felt refreshed, so good and free.

He told me of His Master Plan,
Designed before the world began.
He showed me mysteries and more,
Then baptized me beside the shore.

I now felt called, redeemed, and clean,
Because His face could now be seen.
And there within the holy place,
The Blood of Jesus did erase
The sins which said, "You cannot stand
Within the gates, God's holy land."

I now could gaze within those eyes
Which held my tears and heard my cries.
The Lamb of God, so tenderly,
Had paid the price for you and me.

Set Free

God's Spirit moved within my soul,
For Jesus died and made me whole.
My friend still struggled with his life,
Until the Savior took his strife.

I preached the gospel everywhere.
I did not worry, did not care.
The Holy Ghost encased my soul.
While Christ the Savior made me whole.

I read my Bible every day,
To see what Jesus Christ would say.
And there within the secret place,
I knew my sins God did erase.

My chains fell off, God set me free.
For Jesus died at Calvary.
And when the Prince of Peace did rise,
I saw His Glory in the skies.

God sent His Son to set us free—
Both now and for eternity.
The pearly gates will open wide,
And now in Him I will abide.

Free

He bled and died at Calvary,
That's where my Savior set me free.
Then on the third day as He said,
His body rose out from the dead.

The sky grew deep, the thunder roared,
While angels sang in one accord.
The winds were fierce while up ahead,
I saw the living and the dead.

The born-again were dressed in white,
While infidels were dark as night.
Still, Jesus came to set us free,
Both now and for eternity.

He won the battle that was sure,
With Godly soldiers white and pure.
The Son of God is never late.
So come to Him, don't hesitate.

He Arose

People said that Jesus died—
But that don't tell the story.
On the third day He arose—
Ascended up to Glory.

If you call on Jesus name,
And ask Him to come in—
He will hear and answer you—
Forgiving you from sin.

All your guilt and shame will flee—
You'll feel so clean inside.
God's Spirit reigns eternally,
In Christ you will abide.

He'll take you by His nail-pierced hands—
And hold you oh so tight.
And as you walk close by His side—
He'll take away your night.

Yes, Jesus died upon the cross—
He paid for all our sin.
So, if you want to know Him more—
Just ask the Savior in.

Eternity

He hung upon the bloody tree,
Where Jesus shed His blood for me.
He cleansed me from all sin and shame,
That I might live through Jesus' name.

My friends still mocked the King of Kings,
Who gave His all—new life He brings;
So, hell would not with fires hot—
Consume the sinners on the spot.

He wore sharp thorns upon His head.
While multitudes yelled, Is He dead?
Still, John stood by his Savior's side—
He did not cower, run, or hide.

Christ finished all He came to do,
His death gave life to me and you.
And now He sits at God's right hand,
So, you and I might understand.

That Jesus paid the utmost cost,
Until the devil knew he lost.
For now Eternal Life is free,
Because He died and lives for me.

Redeemer

I saw my Redeemer all bloody and torn—
He hung on the cross while the soldiers did scorn.
He did not yell back, no, He only did pray
That God would forgive them on that gruesome day.

He asked God the Father, why He was forsaken;
And why they cast lots as His clothing was taken.
He cried out, "Forgive them for they do not know,
The reason I'm dying, for I love them so."

The crowd kept on scoffing while innocent blood,
Flowed out of His veins like Gaza's, flash flood.
And there by His mother and John, His dear friend,
He bowed down His head, Our Redeemer was dead.

They buried Him quickly until the third day,
Christ Jesus arose as the Truth, Life, and Way.
I now am redeemed by the Blood of the Lamb.
Because He is risen, forever, I Am.

He will Abide

The sinless Man upon the cross,
Gave up His Life, He suffered loss;
That you and I would be set free.
He did all this for you and me.

And as He said, He will abide—
Through darkness deep, He's by your side.
Just call upon the Savior's name—
He'll save your soul, that's why He came.

For on the cross He overcame,
Our sin and sickness, Fear and shame.
The time is coming to an end,
Still, Jesus Christ will be our friend.

Transformation

My body was jaded, my soul tired too,
When all of a sudden, I ran into You.
Your hair looked like copper; your eyes matched the skies—
A white robe that glistened with gold-colored ties.

You sat down beside me with fresh loaves and fish,
That ever so kindly you put on a dish.
Your Presence revived me, your touch made me whole—
And there, deep inside me your life saved my soul.

You said, "I'll be with you from morning 'till night,
Perfecting my glory, replacing my sight."
Let's walk back together—Now joined side by side,
And strengthened forever, The Groom and His Bride.

Made Whole

I went into the church one day,
And there I knelt down low to pray.
I heard a voice say, "Do not fear,
I am not far, but very near."

I turned to see the angels white,
And Christ my Savior pure and bright.
He called to me, I took His hand,
I knew that God did understand.

He took away my guilt and shame,
I now was free, In Jesus name.
He brought me to my trysting place,
For by His hand He did erase,

The burden which encased my soul,
Could not be found, Christ made me whole.
And there my Savior full of grace,
Showed me the splendor of God's face.

Draw

Draw me fast and draw me near.
Take away my every fear.
On the mountain way up high,
You ascended in the sky.

Let me see your eyes so deep.
Keep me close to your own sheep.
Let me hear the shepherds voice—
Help me make your holy choice.

You have died to set me free.
Now I'll live eternally.
Show me Lord that sacred place—
You forgave all sin, disgrace.

When you draw me, I will be,
By your side eternally.
Up the mountain, through the gates
Peace at last, no more debates.

Truth

I did not know which way to turn,
I still had oh so much to learn.
Then suddenly I felt a hand
And I began to understand.

A voice of truth said, "Follow Me"
And there I saw the crystal sea.
The pearly gates, and streets of gold,
Were full of people—none were old.

While angels sang all dressed in white,
My eyes beheld this glorious sight.
The Father, Son, and Holy Ghost
Unveiled the Truth I needed most.

Until my mind was filled with Light—
Beholding such a glorious sight.
I must go back to where I came—
No longer did my heart feel shame.

The Bible is God's Word to me,
I once was blind but now, I see.
The Truth has made my spirit whole,
And I feel victory in my soul.

Finished

Jesus hung upon a tree—
Shed His blood on Calvary.
Said a prayer for all to hear—
Everyone, both far and near.

Father please forgive them all—
Heal their sins when ere they call.
Make them new in every way.
Turn their darkest night to day.

Mother stay with John, for he
Loves me most, of that, you'll see.
Thunder filled the place where He
Shed His blood for you and me.

Christ our Savior gave His all—
Freeing us from Adam's fall.
Just repent and let Him in—
He will free you from all sin.

It is Finished

I cannot go back in time,
Erase bad choices that were mine.
The only thing which, I can do
Is make things right from me to you.

Whatever happened years ago,
Seemed full of strife, sadness, and woe.
I could not comprehend the "Why?"
Which sadly made my spirit cry.

I thought we could forget the past,
Since time went by and now, at last,
I stood before you, aged and lost—
But still I knew Christ paid the cost.

And while I stood there, heart in hand.
The Savior said, I understand.
For on the cross my pain diminished,
For I remembered—It is finished.

Grace

Grace enables me to say,
I will follow every day.
She's my true enabling friend,
Who carries me from start to end.

I don't deserve this song of praise,
Through dark of night and sunny days.
I could not pay, for grace is free—
To lift me up eternally.

To see me through my hopeless hour,
That's full of mercy, strength, and power.
Now Jesus said, I paid it all—
I will not let my weak ones fall.
Just call upon My holy name,
And grace will free you from all shame.

Lost

I could not find the narrow way,
Until my night was turned to day.
For there I saw the Savior bleed
At Calvary where I was freed.

Then suddenly I saw a sight—
It turned my darkness into Light.
The Light of Life enveloped me,
For Jesus Christ had set me free.

I now was found by God's dear Son,
Who shed His blood and made me one.
The Father, Son, and Holy Ghost,
Drew all mankind from coast to coast.

The Savior gave His all and more,
So, if you hear Him at your door
Just call upon His holy name,
And you will never be the same.

Corn of Wheat

I dropped to my knees
Where He hung on the cross,
And there I did weep
For He suffered great loss.

He bled and He died
But I did not know, why?
My Savior was sinless,
Oh, how I did cry.

Then Jesus looked down
Where He saw a sad sight,
As John His disciple
Remained through the night.

And Mary His mother
Could not understand,
The reason they killed
Such an innocent man.

There was no relief
For it was preordained
That Christ would reverse
All my sickness and pain.

He said, "It is finished."
He could not do more,
But carried me into
A room called, restore.

He now lives inside me—
The Way, Truth, and Life,
Forever will guide me
And heal all my strife.

I'm Saved

I know I'm saved in Jesus' name—
The Bible says, He's still the same.
He died upon the rugged cross,
To save my soul and pay the cost,

For all my sickness, sin, and shame—
His agony became my gain.
His life was sinless, pure, and whole—
And that is why He saved my soul.

I could not pay the price for I,
Had sinned profusely that is why,
Dear God the Father sent His Son—
His blood was shed for everyone.

I heard the gospel, God's good news,
Could not be meddled or diffused.
The Blood of Jesus, God's own Son,
Redeemed my life by what was done.

The Seals

Within the seals of mystery,
My Savior foretold history.
But then He locked them up in time—
The Light of Life arose sublime.

The awe-inspiring script must wait
For golden streets and pearly gates,
Before it's secrets manifest —
The sons of God with white, light, dress.

The Book of Daniel placed each seal
Inside the gates within the wheel.
While Jesus rode a strapping horse—
To win the war, He stayed the course.

The trumpets sounded far and wide
Until we reached the other side.
A place where Zion held the Throne
For God had triumphed on His own.

With manifested sons in Glory
Faultless Lamb — The gospel story,
All God's mysteries now told—
In the end-time they unfold.

Holy Spirit

Holy Spirit comfort me,
And set my inner burdens free.
I know You care, and understand,
So, stay beside me—hand in hand.

I need direction, help me hear,
Your voice of victory—Drawing near.
And when I stand before God's throne,
Please let me know I'm not alone.

I need perception from above,
Where I'm surrounded by God's Love.
I need to call on Jesus' name,
Forgiving me of all my shame.

The Savior sent the Holy Ghost,
So, I would know God loved me most.
For there within God's Holy Place—
I found completion, face to face.

Waiting

Are you waiting for the King?
Do you hear all heaven sing?
Have you asked the Holy One,
If God's work on earth is done?

Can He use you in this hour,
While He fills you with His power?
Have you heard the trumpet blast,
Raising up the first and last?

Wait before the God above,
Full of mercy, grace, and love.
Jesus rides upon His horse,
Showing us the gospel course.

Aba Father—Adonai,
You are watching from up high.
Jesus Christ, you raised your sword—
For you are the risen Lord.

I am waiting for the sound,
Gathering God's children round.
Soon we will no longer wait,
Our eyes will see the golden gate.

His Call

I walked through creeks and meadows fair,
While angels danced just everywhere.
And there I sat to rest a spell,
For where I was, I could not tell.

I heard a voice call out my name,
It was so real and not a game.
And while I waited in that place.
I saw the Glory on His face.

Then suddenly He called my name,
And I no longer felt deep shame.
His voice was gentle, sweet, and kind,
It generated peace of mind.

While all my sickness, sin, and pain,
Fell off of me in Jesus name.
I answered "Lord, what should I do?
The day is dark, and I need You!"

He spoke a Word into my heart,
Reminding me, He would not part.
And there beside the crystal sea,
I knew why God had chosen me.

Christ, Cross, Cornerstone

My heart was aching for the past,
Until I realized things don't last.
The places where I once did tread,
Were overgrown with grass, now dead.

So deep within my soul I cried,
For all the beauty that had died.
Then suddenly I saw the cross,
Where Christ my Savior suffered loss.

And there before me stood a man,
Who gave me grace to understand.
The Blood of Jesus paid the price,
For every sin and all my vice.

The Holy Ghost would settle me,
With love divine eternally.
And I would never be afraid,
Because the debt of sin was paid.

The land now sparkled through the Son,
Who set me free and made me one.
Restoring all that once was lost,
The cornerstone became the cross.

Emmaus Road

I traveled down Emmaus road
And thought of everything
The Master said and now was dead
Where angel choirs Sing.

He taught me how to pray each day—
He said, I must Forgive.
And that He was the Truth, the Way—
He died that I might live.

He said He suffered for all my sins,
For all my sickness too.
He said He's coming back again.
And that He'll see you through.

Just then I looked and saw a man,
All glistening and bright.
He said He was the Word of God,
And spoke of Christ all night.

His Words were powerful and sure—
They touched my heart and soul.
And when He gazed into my eyes,
I felt so loved and whole.

He said that He was coming back,
To resurrect His Bride.
And win the battle with His saints—
I saw that He had cried.

I never will forget this man,
I knew He saved the lost.
And through the darkest night
He came, and paid the highest cost.

Alone

Alone in the city I stumbled and fell.
Then called out to Jesus to save me from hell.
And there as I cried out, I saw a great light,
That shined on the sidewalk—So brilliant and bright.

He reached for my arm and then lifted me high.
I knew it was Jesus then started to cry.
I never will leave you; I'll always be near—
I'll stay right beside you, revoking all fear.

My body felt stronger, He made me feel new—
Then left with a promise for me and for you:
"You're never alone for my Spirit resides,
Within you forever; you're safe by my side."

Agape

The Love of God will pierce your soul,
And touch your being head to toe.
Agape Love heals every sin,
So Jesus Christ can enter in.

Before the world was set in space,
God, Elohim, prepared a place.
Yahweh ordained that you would be,
His own throughout eternity.

For perfect Love cast out all fear,
Proclaiming heaven's atmosphere.
Through every stormy path I trod,
I felt the Presence of our God.

Reborn, redeemed, He paid the cost.
Christ's blood made sure I was not lost.
Agape Love so high and sure,
Brought me to God and made me pure.

Sonship

I traveled back to Romans eight,
Where sons of God did aggregate.
Then back again Isaiah saw,
The Glory Cloud immerse them all.

In bringing many sons to Glory—
Adonai, would tell the story,
Of the Son of God who came,
Healing all in Jesus name.

'Till, He died, and rose to Life—
He forgave my sin and strife.
Through the valley darkness fell,
We're redeemed from death and hell.

Overcomers, glorified,
As we scan the other side,
Every dry bone heard God's call,
For the Savior raised them all.

Sons of God

Sons of God arise today
As overcomers, lead the way.
Transformed by the Spirit's Love—
With impartations from above.

Never more to leave His care—
Jesus Christ is always there.
Dealings from the Lord set straight
Through rough waters, navigate.

As I swim through Romans 8,
I land on verse 28.
Sons of God, your time has come—
Full of Glory, everyone

Hear the trumpets overhead—
While the Bride in white is led—
Guiding all who heed the call—
Christ in me, my All in All.

I Will Restore

This house, it once was newly painted
With flowers placed in perfect array,
And people passing by would smile
With nods of approval day by day.

Today the paint is cracked and worn,
The flowers overcome with weeds,
And every passerby will frown
In contemplation of its needs.

You might be thinking,
"I'm this house, I used to stand erect and strong,
And now when people look my way
They see that there is something wrong."

But listen now to what I say –
A word of hope, of life and more,
As Jesus looked upon your house
I heard Him say, "I will Restore."

"I will rebuild this house again,
A strong foundation shall be laid;
Its beauty will surpass the old
And tearful memories will fade."

I saw Him smile at your house
As if it still was bright and new,
Then Joyfully He spoke these words,
"I'll live within this house with you."

Pain

When Jesus suffered on the cross,
He bore my sickness, pain, and loss.
He took my hurt upon the tree,
Because He loved and cared for me.

He asked the Father, "Why, oh why?"
He suffered so and soon would die
The Father did not say a word
Although, the Savior's cry was heard.

And as He bowed His head and died,
I heard His mother, Mary, cried.

Before the earth was put in place,
And galaxies filled outer space,
God took my suffering, healed my pain--
Forgave my sin, In Jesus name.

Name

Your name is written in His book—
God told me so, just take a look.
And call on Jesus, He will save
You from all sin, that's why He gave,

His Son to die on Calvary—
Forgive our sins and set us free.
The name of Jesus will prevail,
Through every dark and stormy vale.

So, if you called upon His name,
You never more will be the same,
You'll live in heaven evermore,
Because our Savior is the door.

He calls your name and hopes you hear,
That He is standing, Oh so near.
He sees your name and knows your heart—
That's why He called you from the start.

The Valley

Many, even today, are in the valley, but do not talk about it. It takes courage to suffer silently—yet, so many do. And what I'm about to say, probably won't make much sense to you. Nevertheless, it needs to be said.

If you've called on Jesus name, and given your life to God, then you will embark on a journey, which will sometimes be painful, sometimes glorious, but always a necessity. At each demarcation, you can tell the Lord that you've had enough, and yes, He will let you out—away from your upsetting path. But soon you will realize that you no longer sense God's Presence, and that the ease you now experience did, in fact, abort the process of your spiritual transformation. A high price, you might think. Yes!! Too high to measure as now you walk alone and realize that you did not fight the good fight of faith.

I like the McKameys song about the valley of which one verse goes like this:

Life is easy, when you're up on the mountain,
And you've got peace of mind,
Like you've never known
But, then things change and you're down in the valley,
Don't lose faith, for you're never alone.

May we remember those who have gone before us: Daniel was thrown into the lion's den for his faithfulness to God. But the Lord delivered him out, just at the right time. And how can we forget, Shadrach, Meshach, and Abednego, who were thrown into the fiery furnace for obeying God rather than man. Again, in God's time He delivered them and they came forth without even the smell of fire on them. And Joseph and Job and so many others who believed God in the valley until they were delivered when God said, "enough!"

So, my fellow journeyman, you can perceive that no matter what you are experiencing, the Lord has your best interest in hand. Nothing can bypass His watchful eye.

Yes, I was led into the valley many times, but every time one thing was sure—God had His eye on the clock. And when I came forth, I was closer to God and more like Jesus, each and every time.

So keep the faith my friend. Keep your eyes on the goal, and in God's timetable, you will be made complete, entire, and whole. He is faithful and true—yes, our God will never fail you!

CPSIA information can be obtained
at www.ICGtesting.com
Printed in the USA
LVHW030358090222
710663LV00002B/71